The Civil Rights Movement

Michael Anderson

Heinemann Library
Chicago, Illinois

© 2004 Reed Educational & Professional Publishing
Published by Heinemann Library,
an imprint of Reed Educational & Professional Publishing,
Chicago, Illinois

Customer Service 888-454-2279

Visit our website at www.heinemannlibrary.com

Designed by Herman Adler Design
Printed in the United States by Lake Book Manufacturing, Inc.

08 07 06 05 04
10 9 8 7 6 5 4 3 2 1

Library of Congress Cataloging-in-Publication Data
Anderson, Michael, 1972-
   The Civil Rights Movement / Michael Anderson.
        v. cm. — (20th century perspectives)
Includes bibliographical references and index.
Contents: What is the Civil Rights Movement? — A Movement many years in the making — Early steps — Dashed hopes — The first victories — Resistance to the Brown ruling — Bus boycott in Montgomery — Martin Luther King Jr. and nonviolent protest — Central High School in Little Rock — Sit-ins and SNCC — Freedom rides — Birmingham — Political responses to the Movement — March on Washington and the Civil Rights Act — Struggle in Mississippi — Selma and the Voting Rights Act — Civil rights and the arts — A new direction — Other civil rights struggles — The Movement continues — Timeline.
   ISBN 1-4034-3805-6 (library binding-hardcover) — ISBN 1-4034-4179-0 (pbk.)
   1. African Americans—Civil rights—History—20th century—Juvenile literature. 2. Civil rights movements—United States—History—20th century—Juvenile literature. 3. United States—Race relations—Juvenile literature. [1. African Americans—Civil rights—History—20th century. 2. Civil rights movements. 3. Race relations.] I. Title. II. Series.
   E185.61.A56 2003
   323.1'196073—dc21
                                    2003009553

Acknowledgments
The author and publisher are grateful to the following for permission to reproduce copyright material: pp.4, 11, 13, 16, 18, 21, 27, 30, 34, 38(m-l), 40, 41, 43 AP/Wide World; pp. 5, 26, 39 Flip Schulke/Corbis; pp. 6, 7, 12(b-l), 14, 15, 17, 20, 25, 29, 31, 33, 35, 36, 38(b-l) Bettmann/Corbis; p. 8 The Crisis Magazine; p. 9 Shomburg Center for Research in Black Culture/NYPL; p. 10 Brown Brothers; p. 12(t-l) Corbis; p. 19 Hulton Archive by Getty Images; p. 22 Jack Moebes/Corbis; p. 23 Jimmy Ellis/The Tennessean, Nashville; p. 24 David Dennis/Time & Life Pictures/Getty Images; p. 28 Joseph Schwartz Collection/Corbis; p. 32 Michael Abramson/Time & Life Pictures/Getty Images; p. 37(r-t) Sogolonarchives.com, (r-b) Bradley Smith/Corbis; p. 42 Wally McNamee/Corbis

Cover photo reproduced with permission of Flip Schulke/Corbis

Every effort has been made to contact copyright holders of any material reproduced in this book. Any omissions will be rectified in subsequent printings if notice is given to the publisher.

Contents

What Is the Civil Rights Movement?

The United States had never seen a gathering like it. On August 28, 1963, more than 250,000 people came together in the nation's capital, Washington, D.C. There were African Americans and whites, young and old, celebrities and ordinary people. In front of the Lincoln Memorial, they listened to speeches and joined together in song. The event, called the March on Washington, was one of the first to be broadcast live on television around the world.

The purpose of the march was to call attention to the cause of civil rights. Civil rights are the freedoms given to citizens by their government. In the United States, the idea of civil rights was central to the founding of the nation and its government. The people of the American colonies chose to break away from Great Britain in 1776 because they felt that the British government was not respecting their rights. In the Declaration of Independence, the colonists stated "that all men are created equal, that they are endowed [provided something freely] by their Creator with certain unalienable [permanent] rights." By this they meant that people had rights that their government could not take away from them. When the time came to create a constitution for the new United States, the people made sure to limit the government's power over citizens. The Bill of Rights to the U.S. Constitution spelled out the freedoms of individual citizens that the government had to respect.

Tens of thousands of demonstrators gathered at the Washington Monument at the start of the March on Washington.

The Declaration of Independence and the Constitution earned the United States a reputation as the land of freedom. In reality, however, the country did not always live up to its ideals of freedom and equality. For many years some groups of people had fewer rights and opportunities than other groups. Women, for example, were denied the right to vote and had limited educational and career opportunities. The American Indians had their land taken away as the United States expanded to the west.

Over the years women, American Indians, and other groups have pressured the government for equal treatment. But the push for civil rights is most closely identified with African Americans, or blacks, as they are most commonly called. From the beginning their struggle was unique. No other group of people was brought to the United States in chains and forced into slavery. And no other group was officially defined in the Constitution as something less that human. For purposes of taxation and representation in Congress, a slave was counted as only three-fifths of a person. After slavery ended, blacks were long denied even the most basic rights. They could not vote or attend school where they chose. They were shut out of decent jobs. They could not even eat or get a drink of water at a public fountain unless it was marked "Colored." After enduring such treatment for hundreds of years, black Americans united in the 20th century to fight for equality. Their efforts are known as the civil rights movement.

Many people think of the civil rights movement as an event of the 1950s and 1960s. It is true that most of the historic developments happened during those years. The push for civil rights for black Americans began much earlier, however, and it continues even today.

Two young boys wear sandwich boards at a civil rights march.

A Movement Many Years in the Making

The first ship carrying African slaves from Africa to the American colonies arrived in Virginia in 1619. The spread of slavery in the colonies was slow at first. By the 1660s, however, colonists were bringing in slaves by the thousands. Since slaves were considered to be property, they had few rights. Their inferior status was put into law when the Constitution was approved in 1788.

A source of conflict

Slaves were kept in both the Northern and Southern states, but eventually slavery became much more widespread in the South. The economy of the South relied heavily on the large-scale production of crops such as tobacco, sugar, and cotton. The demand for laborers to work in the fields led to the rapid expansion of slavery. In the North, however, the economy became more dependent on industry, making slavery less valuable economically. At the same time, a growing number of Northerners began voicing the opinion that slavery was wrong. One by one the Northern states passed laws banning slavery.

There were segregated drinking fountains in the South of the United States before the civil rights movement began.

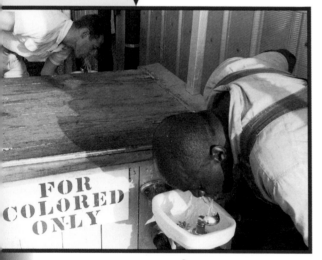

FOR COLORED ONLY

Disagreements over slavery were a major cause of the American Civil War, which began in 1861. The Southern states had withdrawn from the United States because they feared that President Abraham Lincoln would outlaw slavery. In 1862, Lincoln issued the Emancipation Proclamation, which freed the slaves in the Southern states. With the help of many black soldiers, the North won the Civil War in 1865. Soon afterward, Congress passed the 13th amendment, which officially outlawed slavery.

Reconstruction

In the years that followed the Civil War, the United States had to deal with the problems raised by the war. This period is known as Reconstruction. Black Americans made some progress during this time. The 14th Amendment, approved in 1868, declared that former slaves were citizens and entitled to equal treatment under the law. Two years later, the 15th Amendment gave former male slaves the right to vote.

For a time, blacks were able to make good use of their newfound freedom. They were elected to state legislatures and to Congress. The new state lawmakers started public school systems, which finally allowed some blacks to get a good education and advance in society. They became successful doctors, lawyers, teachers, and businesspeople.

Racist violence and Jim Crow

Many Southern whites reacted strongly against the progress of blacks during Reconstruction. They viewed successful blacks as a threat to their way of life. To maintain their sense of superiority over blacks—and the advantages it gave them—they had to stop their progress. One way they did this was through violence. Many of the people behind the violence belonged to a terrorist organization called the Ku Klux Klan, which was formed in 1865. Blacks who tried to register to vote were threatened, beaten, or shot. Hundreds of blacks were murdered in the South each year. By the 1890s, crowds of people throughout the South were gathering to watch blacks being tortured, burned, or hanged. This type of violence was called lynching.

Ida B. Wells (1862 – 1931) was one of the first civil rights leaders. At first a teacher and later a journalist, she courageously spoke out against the lynching, segregation, and racial inequality in the South.

Along with violence and terror, white Southerners also used the law against blacks. Some states had no intention of following the amendments that ordered them to treat blacks as equals. When the last federal troops left the South in 1877, Southern governments quickly fell back under the control of racist whites. Local communities introduced laws to segregate, or keep apart, blacks and whites. In public places and on public transportation, signs reading "White" and "Colored" identified seats and facilities reserved for each race. These Jim Crow laws, as they were called, came to control virtually every part of life in the South.

Backward steps

By the 1890s, most of the gains that blacks had made during Reconstruction had disappeared. Most blacks were poor because of job discrimination—whites would not hire them for good jobs. Many were forced to become sharecroppers, meaning they worked on land owned by whites in return for a small portion of the crop. Their living conditions were little better than slavery. Public schools for blacks were either nonexistent or rundown. In addition, Southern states made it more difficult for blacks to vote. One method was requiring blacks to pass nearly impossible tests before they could register to vote.

In 1896, the U.S. Supreme Court officially supported segregation in a case called *Plessy v. Ferguson*. The Court ruled that segregation was legal as long as "separate but equal" facilities were available for blacks and whites. "Separate but equal" would be the law of the land for nearly 60 years.

Early Steps

By 1900, black Americans were in worse shape than they had been since the days of slavery. Growing numbers of Northern whites had begun to agree with Southern arguments that blacks were inferior. The Supreme Court's decision in the *Plessy* case reflected the nation's widespread belief that segregation was best for both whites and blacks.

Washington and Du Bois

Some blacks responded to the deepening of white supremacy by promoting the idea of accommodation. Instead of working to end segregation, these blacks accepted it. Their goal was to improve their lives within the segregated system. The leader of this group was Booker T. Washington. A former slave, Washington headed a school in Alabama called the Tuskegee Institute. He urged blacks to better themselves by learning trades and farming skills. Washington was the best-known black leader in the country in the early 20th century.

Other blacks strongly rejected the idea of accommodation. They believed that the only way to better their situation was to protest. Their goal was nothing less than the end of racial segregation, discrimination, and violence. From the time that Jim Crow laws were introduced, some blacks had resisted them. They held rallies, filed lawsuits, and organized boycotts against segregated streetcars. But only in the early 20th century did blacks begin to join together on a large scale to push for civil rights. The most famous leader of this group was W.E.B. Du Bois. He believed that higher education and the right to vote were key to the advancement of black Americans.

The Niagara Movement

In the summer of 1905, Du Bois organized a conference of black professionals at Niagara Falls, New York. Among the 29 men who took part were doctors, teachers, lawyers, and journalists. The Niagara Movement, as it became known, was the first organization to insist that blacks be given all the rights promised to citizens in the Constitution. The group issued a declaration that called for full civil rights for blacks as well as the end of all racial discrimination.

Southern mobs, with local authorities seldom trying to stop them, lynched over 3000 African Americans from the 1890s through the 1930s. This 1937 cartoon says that Congress therefore needed to make anti-lynching a matter of national law.

Remember Me, Mister?

ANTI LYNCHING BILL

SPECIAL SESSION

THE SENATE

Courtesy Baltimore S[...]

We claim for ourselves every single right that belongs to a freeborn American, political, civil, and social; and until we get these rights we will never cease to protest and assail [attack] the ears of America. The battle we wage is not for ourselves alone but for all true Americans. It is a fight for ideals, lest this, our common fatherland, false to its founding, become in truth the land of the thief and the home of the slave.

—W.E.B. Du Bois, from a speech given at the second meeting of the Niagara Movement in August 1906

The founding members of the Niagara Movement posed for this picture at Niagara Falls. W.E.B. Du Bois is second from the right in the middle row.

After the first meeting, the Niagara Movement expanded to include about 30 branches. The group continued to meet each year. But the movement never succeeded in organizing protests on a massive scale. It was weakened by a shortage of funds and by conflicts among its leaders. The movement's lack of white members also kept it from attracting widespread support. This last weakness was remedied when a new civil rights group was founded in 1909.

NAACP

That year, a group of well-educated, successful Americans met in New York City for the National Conference on the Negro. The conference was organized in response to the lynchings of two blacks in Springfield, Illinois, in 1908. Among the participants were blacks from the Niagara Movement, as well as concerned whites. The reason for the conference was to discuss ways to end racial discrimination and segregation. The meeting led to the creation of the National Association for the Advancement of Colored People (NAACP).

The NAACP decided to push for civil rights through lawsuits, not protests. By challenging unfair practices in court, the group hoped to bring about the passage of more just laws. Arguing before the Supreme Court, the NAACP won early victories against discrimination in voting and housing. For decades, however, the NAACP's legal victories would have little effect on the lives of most blacks.

Dashed Hopes

In the early decades of the 20th century, many blacks gave up on the South. They saw little hope for achieving social and political equality, and many even feared for their lives. Eventually hundreds of thousands of these blacks would leave the Southern states for the North. What they found in their new home, though, was often disappointing.

Great Migration

The movement of blacks northward was slow at first. In 1915, however, their numbers began to grow dramatically. At the time, World War I was raging in Europe and U.S. factories were flooded with orders for supplies. The promise of factory jobs lured tens of thousands of blacks to Northern cities such as New York, Chicago, Detroit, and Philadelphia. Between 1910 and 1920, some 500,000 blacks went north. Even greater numbers followed in the next decade. This mass movement became known as the Great Migration.

Their experiences in the North were mixed. Often they were able to lead a better life than they had in the South. Many found decent jobs, and they were paid more fairly for their work. They were much freer to vote as well. But they also found that racism was not only a Southern problem. Many Northern whites resisted the movement of blacks into their communities. They feared that the newcomers would compete with them for housing, jobs, and political power. In 1919, racial tensions led to riots and lynchings in dozens of cities in both the North and South. Because of the widespread violence, this time is remembered as the Red Summer.

An African American factory worker oversees the pouring of molten steel around the time of World War I.

Disappointment

Many Northern whites began to believe that segregation was the only way to keep peace between the races. Real estate companies sold houses to blacks only in certain parts of cities, leading to the development of all-white and all-black neighborhoods. The black areas, which came to be known as ghettos, were often overcrowded and rundown. As the neighborhoods became segregated, schools followed the same pattern. Discrimination grew in the workplace as well, as companies refused to hire blacks for the best jobs.

Whites also became more strongly opposed to civil rights activism during this period. The NAACP experienced tremendous growth during the war years, especially in the South. This changed after a NAACP leader was severely beaten by a gang of whites in Austin, Texas, in 1919. This incident, along with a return of the Ku Klux Klan, led to a great decrease in NAACP membership throughout the South. Many people decided that belonging to the group was too risky.

Support for segregation

During this difficult time, many black Americans turned to a new leader. Marcus Garvey, an immigrant from Jamaica, delivered a different message from what blacks had been hearing from the NAACP. Instead of pushing for integration, Garvey supported segregation. He told blacks that they should take pride in their African heritage, and he spread the idea that black Americans should create their own nation in Africa. By the early 1920s his organization, the United Negro Improvement Association, had several hundred thousand members. Garvey's following declined, however, after he was jailed for mail fraud in 1925. Two years later, U.S. officials forced him to return to Jamaica.

With powerful speeches and a unique appearance, Marcus Garvey rallied blacks more effectively than the NAACP did during the 1920s.

Even at the height of his popularity, Garvey caused sharp disagreement. Other black leaders, including W.E.B. Du Bois, feared that he would hurt their efforts to gain racial equality for blacks. Yet in the following years, even more blacks came to agree with Garvey's idea that segregation might be in their best interest. Racial violence, the growth of ghettos, and job discrimination continued. The NAACP's work still was not making much of a difference in people's everyday lives. Under these conditions, many blacks accepted segregation. In the 1930s even Du Bois came around to this way of thinking. After criticizing the NAACP's goal of integration as unrealistic, he left the organization in 1934.

A victory for women

While African Americans lost ground in the early 20th century, women made progress in winning rights. Their biggest victory came in the area of voting. Women began working for full voting rights in the mid-19th century. The leaders of the movement in its early decades were Elizabeth Cady Stanton and Susan B. Anthony. Gradually some states gave women the right to vote. The movement gained momentum during World War I, when thousands of women volunteered to help the war effort. Women finally won full voting rights when the 19th Amendment to the Constitution became law on August 26, 1920.

The First Victories

Although some blacks supported the idea of segregation, many began to resist it more strongly in the 1940s and 1950s. The Supreme Court's 1896 decision in the *Plessy v. Ferguson* case had said that segregation was legal as long as separate facilities for blacks and whites were of similar quality. The reality, however, was that black schools, housing, and other facilities were rarely equal to the white ones.

World War II and after

The push for equal treatment gained force because of World War II. Both the industries that produced war supplies and the armed services themselves were segregated. In 1941 a black union leader named A. Philip Randolph planned a huge march in Washington, D.C., to protest discrimination in the war industries. Before the march could even take place, President Franklin D. Roosevelt agreed to ban discrimination in defense industries and government.

Black U.S. Air Force pilots kneel beside the aircraft Skipper's Darlin' in Italy during World War II.

The growing pressure for equal treatment soon began to see results. In 1946 President Harry S. Truman set up a Committee on Civil Rights, the first group of its kind within the federal government. The group's purpose was to protect the civil rights of all Americans. In the same year, the Supreme Court ruled that segregation in transportation between the states was unconstitutional. In 1948, Truman ordered the end of segregation in the military.

Jackie Robinson

Along with most other parts of American life, the sports world was affected by segregation during the Jim Crow era. For years, black baseball players were not allowed to play in the major leagues. They could play only in the separate Negro Leagues. In the 1940s, however, the team president of the Brooklyn Dodgers, Branch Rickey, decided to challenge segregation in the majors. In 1945 he gave a contract to a black player named Jackie Robinson. After a season in the minor leagues, Robinson was brought up to the majors in 1947. Throughout the season he was taunted and threatened by whites, but he played brilliantly. He was named rookie of the year in 1948 and went on to earn a place in the Baseball Hall of Fame.

School desegregation

The breakthrough of the civil rights struggle came in the area of education. Black leaders such as W.E.B. Du Bois had long believed that schooling was the best way for blacks to improve their situation. Educated blacks better understood what their civil rights were—and when those rights were being ignored. Few blacks, however, were able to get an education that compared to that of whites. In the 1930s, most black schools in the South had no blackboards, libraries, or textbooks. The teachers sometimes knew little more than their students did.

The NAACP began fighting inequality in the schools in the 1930s. At first the group's court victories affected higher education. An important win came in 1950. The Supreme Court ruled that separate schools of higher education were unconstitutional if they did not provide equal learning opportunities for blacks and whites. But the decision did not end the practice of school segregation. As long as equal facilities were available for both races, separation was still legal.

Linda Brown stands in front of Sumner School in Topeka, Kansas, in 1964. The refusal ten years earlier to admit her to the then-segregated school led to an historic court case.

The next step for the NAACP was to challenge segregation itself. The group decided to make the case that separate black and white schools were never truly equal. Their goal was to get black children admitted to white schools. The key court case centered on Linda Brown, a seven-year-old girl living in Topeka, Kansas. The Brown family lived within blocks of a white school, but Linda was forced to attend a black school across town.

NAACP lawyers, led by Thurgood Marshall, argued that school segregation was harming black children. The case, known as *Brown v. Board of Education of Topeka,* went all the way to the Supreme Court. In 1954, the Court decided in favor of the Browns. The Court agreed that segregation was harmful to black children because it creates "a feeling of inferiority as to their status in the community that may affect their hearts and minds in a way unlikely ever to be undone." The ruling went on to state that "separate educational facilities are inherently [by nature] unequal." Nearly 60 years after the *Plessy* decision, the Court finally struck down the idea of "separate but equal."

Resistance to the *Brown* Ruling

Many people consider the *Brown* decision to be the start of the civil rights movement. A major blow to the legal basis for segregation, the ruling encouraged the NAACP to challenge unfair practices in other areas of public life. Lawyers began to file suits against segregation in employment, transportation, housing, public parks, and recreational places such as swimming pools and golf courses. The NAACP was often victorious.

Because the *Brown* ruling was so historic, opposition was strong and swift. Resistance to the ruling was most widespread in the South. Many Southern whites felt that the whole system of segregation—in fact, their whole way of life—was under attack. They argued that states had the right to run their schools however they wanted. The federal government, they said, had no authority to interfere. With this idea in mind, they disobeyed the ruling in a number of ways.

An angry mother leads her child away from a newly segregated school in Birmingham, Alabama.

Delaying tactics

The opponents of school integration had one important thing in their favor: the *Brown* decision did not set a timetable for school desegregation. A follow-up ruling in 1955 stated only that schools must desegregate "with all deliberate speed." In many places, school officials admitted black students quickly. In other places, school boards opposed to integration used the Court's vague language to their advantage. With no firm deadline to meet, they sometimes delayed integration for years.

Southern states also responded to the *Brown* ruling with political and legal moves of their own. State lawmakers gave local school boards the authority to close down their schools rather than integrate them. They encouraged whites to set up all-white private schools. Yet another strategy in some places was to increase funding for black schools to raise them to the level of white schools. The lawmakers hoped that if the schools really did become equal, then they would not have to integrate them.

White Citizens Councils

Along with school boards and politicians, ordinary Southerners banded together to oppose integration. Just months after the *Brown* ruling, a group called the White Citizens Council was formed in Mississippi. Soon, Citizens Councils spread to Alabama, Louisiana, Georgia, Texas, and other states. The councils claimed to be more respectable than the Ku Klux Klan. They said they would fight integration in legal ways only. In reality, however, many council members were also members of the Klan and other violent groups.

The White Citizens Councils had different strategies to fight desegregation. Council members fired or refused to do business with blacks and whites who signed petitions, statements of support, in favor of desegregation. Business owners refused to give the petitioners credit, which many depended on to get food and clothing. Council members also used threats and terror to achieve their goals. Black students were often turned away when they tried to enter all-white public schools. In some cases, white violence forced black students to return to all-black schools.

Federal inaction

The federal government did little to stop Southerners in their resistance. Federal courts supported the ruling, but they also accepted Southern delays. The result was that school desegregation happened very slowly. Without strong federal support, the ruling was something of a disappointment.

Members of a White Citizens Council gather to protest against school integration in New Orleans, Louisiana.

Black Monday

"Black Monday" is the name coined by Representative John Bell Williams of Mississippi to designate Monday, May 17th, 1954, a date long to be remembered throughout the nation. . . "Black Monday," is indeed symbolic of the date. Black denoting darkness and terror. Black signifying the absence of light and wisdom. Black embodying grief, destruction, and death."

—Judge Tom Brady, a leader of the White Citizens Council movement

Bus Boycott in Montgomery

For many blacks, the failure of the *Brown* ruling to bring about meaningful change meant that they needed to fight segregation in new ways. They started to think that the NAACP's strategy of depending on court rulings was ineffective. Some blacks decided to challenge segregation more directly. They won their first major victory in the city of Montgomery, Alabama, in 1955.

Segregation in public transportation

Of all the areas in which Southern blacks had been forced to put up with segregation, public transportation was among the most bothersome. Because few blacks could afford to own cars, they were the majority of the passengers on buses in many cities. But blacks had to sit in the back of the bus because the front was reserved for whites. If the white section filled up, the driver could force an entire row of black passengers to stand to make room for the next white person who boarded. In some cities, blacks were not even allowed to walk through the white section to get to their seats. They had to pay their fare in the front of the bus and then get off and enter through the rear door.

Rosa Parks being fingerprinted after her arrest for refusing to give up her bus seat to a white passenger.

An historic decision

On December 1, 1955, a 42-year-old black woman named Rosa Parks boarded a bus to go home from her job at a department store in downtown Montgomery, Alabama. She took a seat in the middle of the bus, just behind the white passengers. As the bus filled up, the driver noticed a white man standing. He ordered Parks and the rest of the black passengers in her row to stand. Three of the passengers obeyed and moved to the back of the bus, but Parks refused. The driver called the police, and she was arrested. Parks was a well-respected member of the black community in Montgomery. She was the secretary of the local NAACP. News of her arrest spread quickly. After getting her out of jail, NAACP leaders asked Parks if she was willing to fight the charges against her. She said yes.

Boycott

Parks' decision excited the city's opponents of segregation. Some of them decided to protest against her arrest and trial by organizing a boycott of the city's buses. When the bus company lost most of its customers, they hoped, it would be forced to change its policies.

On the morning of the boycott, the organizers were thrilled. The buses were nearly empty. That afternoon black leaders formed a protest organization called the Montgomery Improvement Association (MIA). The group elected a young minister named Martin Luther King Jr. as its leader. The MIA decided to continue the boycott.

Montgomery's blacks supported the boycott even though it made their lives even harder. They had depended on the buses to get to work and to school and to do their shopping. Many now had to walk everywhere. Soon, however, the MIA set up a huge carpool. People who owned cars began to give rides to people who needed them. The bus company complained to city officials that it was losing 30,000 to 40,000 fares every day.

As the boycott went on month after month, Montgomery's whites grew angrier. Martin Luther King Jr. received threatening letters and his home was bombed. Police ticketed and arrested carpool drivers. Later, the city called for the arrest of huge numbers of people who were taking part in the boycott. But these efforts only made the boycotters more determined. The mass arrests helped turn the boycott into international news.

This picture shows Rosa Parks riding a bus in Montgomery just after the Supreme Court's ruling against segregation took effect.

Rosa Parks keeps her seat

When the driver saw me still sitting, he asked if I was going to stand up and I said, "No, I'm not."

And he said, "Well, if you don't stand up, I'm going to call the police and have you arrested."

I said, "You may do that."

He did get off the bus, and I still stayed where I was. Two policemen came on the bus. One of the policemen asked me if the bus driver had asked me to stand and I said yes.

He said, "Why don't you stand up?"

And I asked him, "Why do you push us around?"

He said, "I do not know, but the law is the law and you're under arrest."

—Rosa Parks recalls her experience of December 1, 1955

Victory

Seeing the strength of the boycott, the MIA decided to challenge the whole system of bus segregation in federal court. A lawsuit was filed on behalf of Rosa Parks and four other women. In June 1956 a court ruled that bus segregation was unconstitutional. The U.S. Supreme Court agreed. The ruling took effect in December 1956. King and other boycott leaders rode a bus together in triumph.

Martin Luther King Jr. and Nonviolent Protest

The Montgomery bus boycott began a new phase of the civil rights movement. Its success showed people how effective organized, peaceful protest could be. In the following years, the strategy of nonviolence became the focus of the movement. The best-known civil rights leader to spread the idea of nonviolence was Martin Luther King Jr.

Growth of a leader

Born in Atlanta, Georgia, in 1929, King was the son and grandson of Baptist ministers. A gifted student, he entered college when he was only fifteen. Three years later he graduated and entered a seminary to study to become a minister. He graduated from the seminary in 1951 at the top of his class. Then King went to Boston University, where he earned a Ph.D. He became pastor of the Dexter Avenue Baptist Church in Montgomery, Alabama, in 1954.

A year later King showed his leadership skills in the bus boycott. He was a powerful speaker who inspired his listeners with a message of hope. King made Southern blacks believe that change was possible. His trips through the North to raise funds for the boycott earned him respect there as well.

Martin Luther King Jr., right, and Ralph Abernathy, left, lead demonstrators in the march on Birmingham, Alabama, on April 12, 1963.

King's justification

You may well ask, "Why direct action? Why sit-ins, marches and so forth? Isn't negotiation a better path?" You are quite right in calling for negotiation. Indeed, this is the very purpose of direct action. Nonviolent direct action seeks to create such a crisis and foster such a tension that a community which has constantly refused to negotiate is forced to confront the issue. It seeks to so dramatize the issue that it can no longer be ignored.

—Martin Luther King Jr., from "Letter from Birmingham Jail," 1963

Gandhi and the principles of nonviolence

King first read the writings of Mahatma Gandhi while studying to become a minister. Gandhi was the national hero of India. He helped end British rule over his country using only nonviolent methods. His campaign was based on direct action, such as boycotts of British goods. He refused to pay taxes to the British government, and more than once he chose to go to jail rather than obey British laws. His determination and his peaceful ways won him a mass following among the Indian people. Many of his British opponents admired him also. Largely because of Gandhi's efforts, India won independence from Great Britain in 1947.

Gandhi's ideas influenced a number of black leaders in the United States. One of them was James Farmer, who founded the Congress of Racial Equality (CORE) in Chicago in 1942. The group's goal was to end racial discrimination through nonviolence. Farmer and CORE would lead many civil rights protests over the years. But King emerged as the most famous black supporter of Gandhi's ideas. He knew that some whites would respond to the civil rights movement with violence. The bombing of his home during the bus boycott had made that very clear. Yet he told his followers over and over again that they must not answer violence with violence. By refusing to act as intolerantly as their opponents did, they would win people over to their cause—just as Gandhi had in India.

SCLC

In 1957, a group of black ministers from across the South formed a new civil rights organization called the Southern Christian Leadership Conference (SCLC). The group's leaders were King and his close friend Ralph Abernathy, who also had been a key figure in the bus boycott. The SCLC believed that the NAACP's emphasis on lawsuits was narrow and ineffective. Like CORE, it dedicated itself to working for desegregation and civil rights through nonviolent resistance.

Central High School in Little Rock

Classes were scheduled to begin at Central High School in Little Rock, Arkansas, on September 3, 1957. The school was to admit its first black students on that day. Few people expected serious trouble—Arkansas was not considered to be as racist as the states of the Deep South, such as Alabama and Mississippi. In Little Rock, the state capital, public officials had integrated city buses, parks, and other public services and facilities. After the *Brown* decision in 1954, the Little Rock School Board quickly announced that it would obey the ruling.

Elizabeth Eckford is harassed by an angry mob as she arrives alone at Central High School.

The people of Little Rock, however, were another story. Many whites were not happy with the changes that had come to their city. As the opposition grew, the school board put off integration for three years, until 1957. Then, as the date approached, the board took steps to limit the number of black students who were admitted to Central High School. In the end, only nine black students enrolled at the school for the 1957–58 school year.

The governor of Arkansas, Orval Faubus, was very aware of the public's opposition to integration. He was concerned above all with remaining as governor. Up for reelection in 1958, he saw a chance to win votes by openly opposing desegregation. Governor Faubus decided that he would not force integration if the majority of whites was so strongly against it.

Days of tension

On the day before school began in 1957, Governor Faubus announced on television that he would send the Arkansas National Guard to Central High School. He said that the armed soldiers were needed for the protection of the nine black students. Their real job, though, was to keep the black students out of the school. On the first day of classes, the black students stayed home. The school board had told the students to keep away until a legal ruling resolved the issue. That day a federal judge ordered that desegregation of the school must proceed immediately. The black students were told to report to class the next day.

Early the next morning, eight of the black students met at the home of Daisy Bates, the president of the Arkansas branch of the NAACP. Bates planned to drive all nine students to the school as a group. But one of the students, Elizabeth Eckford, never heard of the plan. She arrived at the school alone and was met by National Guardsmen and an angry white mob. From the crowd she heard someone shout, "Lynch her!" Eckford tried to make her way to the school, but she was turned away. The soldiers also forced the other eight students to turn back. Day after day the troops and the mob returned.

An act of defiance

Never before had a governor used state troops to prevent the integration of a school. Governor Faubus was ignoring a federal court order as well. President Eisenhower had hoped to avoid getting involved in the crisis, but the governor's continued disobedience forced him to take action. At a meeting in Rhode Island, Eisenhower told Governor Faubus to obey the court order. After the governor returned to Arkansas, however, the standoff continued.

A week later a federal court ordered Governor Faubus to remove the National Guard from Central High School. This time the governor obeyed. While the troops left, the mobs remained. On September 23, the nine black students slipped into the school under police guard. Outside a riot broke out, with thousands of angry whites attacking news reporters and any blacks they could find.

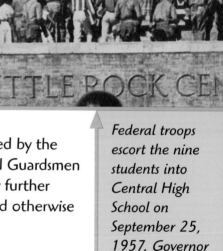

Seeing no other resolution to the conflict, President Eisenhower made the decision to send federal troops to Little Rock. On September 25 the soldiers escorted the black students into Central. After a few days they were replaced by the Arkansas National Guard, now under federal control. National Guardsmen remained at Central for the whole school year, preventing any further violence. But the black students were still taunted, shoved, and otherwise harassed by some white students.

The standoff in Little Rock made Governor Faubus a hero among segregationists. He was easily re-elected in 1958. His success taught other Southern politicians that they could win votes by opposing integration.

Federal troops escort the nine students into Central High School on September 25, 1957. Governor Faubus warned that "blood will run in the streets" if the nine tried to integrate the school.

Ernest Green

Only one of the nine black students who entered Central High School in 1957 was a senior. Here Ernest Green describes his graduation in 1958:

There were a lot of claps for the students. They talked about who had received scholarships, who was an honor student, and all that as they called the names off. When they called my name there was nothing, just the name, and there was this eerie silence. But I figured they didn't have to. Because after I got that diploma, that was it. I had accomplished what I had come there for.

Sit-ins and the SNCC

The events of the 1950s deeply affected young blacks in the South. The courage displayed by the high school students in Little Rock, Arkansas, was particularly inspiring. Earlier, the Montgomery bus boycott had shown them the power of nonviolent protest. In the spirit of the boycott, college students in the South launched a movement of their own in 1960. Their form of protest was known as the sit-in.

The sit-in movement began as a response to segregation at lunch counters. Lunch counters were a popular place for shoppers to take a break and enjoy a meal. Stores were happy to accept money from blacks who wanted to buy merchandise. Lunch counters, though, were only for whites, and black customers could not get even a sandwich or a cup of coffee.

SNCC students protest lunch counter segregation at a Greensboro, North Carolina sit-in in 1960.

Greensboro

On February 1, 1960, four black students from North Carolina Agricultural and Technical College went to the Woolworth's department store in downtown Greensboro. They sat down at the "white" lunch counter and ordered coffee. Although the waitress refused to serve them, the students stayed in their seats. They sat there, quietly studying, until the store closed for the day. When the four students returned to Woolworth's the next day, more students joined them. Their numbers grew each day, and soon the sit-ins spread to other stores.

The students in Greensboro did not invent the sit-in. CORE held the first sit-ins at lunch counters and restaurants in the early 1940s. But it was the Greensboro protest that first grabbed national headlines. Some historians consider the Greensboro sit-in to be the turning point in the civil rights movement. From then on, direct action would be the most important strategy behind the movement. The sit-ins were also the first type of protest to get many young people involved in the struggle.

The movement spreads

Within days, the sit-in movement expanded beyond Greensboro to other cities in North Carolina. Soon sit-ins were taking place in every Southern state. One city that was especially prominent in the movement was Nashville, Tennessee. The year before the Greensboro sit-in, a young black ministry student named James Lawson began holding workshops to teach students about nonviolence. In the workshops, he and the students acted out scenes to practice nonviolent techniques. Some pretended to sit at a lunch counter while others played the role of angry whites.

White men try to violently pull sit-in participants away from a lunch counter in downtown Nashville.

With this training, the Nashville students were well prepared when they began their sit-ins in February 1960. Like the students in other cities, they made sure to dress nicely and be polite. They brought books with them to occupy themselves after they were refused service. Many stores decided to close down their lunch counters rather than serve blacks. Angry whites reacted by shoving the protesters and burning them with cigarettes. They poured ketchup and sugar over their heads. The protesters almost never fought back, but still the police often arrested them for "disorderly conduct" instead of the hostile whites. No matter how many students were arrested, however, there were always more to take their place.

Before long owners of stores targeted by the sit-ins were losing a lot of money. Some became eager to desegregate so their businesses could return to normal. By the end of 1960, stores in more than 80 cities and towns had begun to serve blacks. The lunch counters in Nashville were opened to all in May.

Formation of SNCC

With their dignity and determination, the students of the sit-in movement won many supporters for their cause. Many Northern—and even some Southern—whites expressed admiration for the young activists. The sit-ins also won the support of the NAACP, SCLC, and CORE. The students, however, decided to remain separate from these established organizations.

In April 1960, about 200 student leaders gathered at Shaw University in Raleigh, North Carolina. Among them were both blacks from the South and whites from the North. Together they formed a new group called the Student Nonviolent Coordinating Committee (SNCC) to organize their protests. SNCC's symbol was a black hand clasping a white hand.

The first sit-in

The first sit-in we had was really funny, because the waitresses were nervous. They must have dropped two thousand dollars' worth of dishes that day. It was almost a cartoon. One in particular, she was so nervous, she picked up dishes and she dropped one, and she'd pick up another one, and she'd drop it. It was really funny, and we were sitting there trying not to laugh, because we thought that laughing would be insulting and we didn't want to create that kind of atmosphere. At the same time we were scared to death.

—Diane Nash, a leader of the Nashville sit-ins

Freedom Rides

In November 1960, as sit-ins continued across the South, John F. Kennedy was elected president of the United States. His victory filled many civil rights activists with hope. Kennedy defeated his opponent, Richard Nixon, by a very narrow margin, thanks in large part to the support of black voters. A few months after taking office in 1961, the new president faced his first major civil rights challenge—the Freedom Rides.

The Rides take shape

In 1961 blacks were still treated like second-class citizens when traveling by bus or train between states. Years before, in 1946, the Supreme Court had ruled that segregation in interstate transportation was unconstitutional. Then, in 1960, the Court decided that segregation in bus station waiting rooms and restaurants was unconstitutional as well. Without enforcement, however, the Court rulings were meaningless.

Freedom riders are guarded by two Mississippi National Guardsmen on the way to Montgomery, Alabama, in 1961.

Therefore, CORE decided to test the rulings with events called Freedom Rides. In 1947, CORE sent a group of black and white passengers on a bus trip through the upper South. Half of the riders were arrested, but the ride did not attract as much attention as CORE had wanted. In 1961, the group used the idea of the Freedom Rides to test the new Court ruling on interstate travel. The plan was for blacks and whites to sit together on buses traveling through the South. At each station, the whites would use the "blacks only" facilities and the blacks would use the "whites only" facilities.

First ride

Thirteen Freedom Riders boarded two buses in Washington, D.C., on May 4, 1961. They were bound for New Orleans, Louisiana. Their trip was designed to take them through Georgia, Alabama, and Mississippi—the heart of the Deep South. They were certain before they started that racists would react violently. Yet they hoped above all that their dramatic ride would force the federal government to take action.

As expected, the Freedom Riders faced hostility nearly everywhere they went. The real trouble began in Alabama. On the way from Atlanta, Georgia, to Birmingham, Alabama, the buses stopped in the Alabama town of Anniston. Mobs of angry whites were there to meet them. One of the buses had its windows smashed and its tires slashed. The bus drove on, but the mob followed. Just outside of town, someone in the mob tossed a bomb inside the bus. With the bus in flames, the passengers just barely escaped with their lives.

The passengers on the second bus were brutally beaten first in Anniston and again in Birmingham. Despite the violence, both groups of Freedom Riders wanted to continue their trip. But every bus driver in Birmingham was too afraid to take them. "I have only one life to give," one driver said, "and I'm not going to give it to the NAACP or CORE!" Still under threat, the Freedom Riders decided to fly to New Orleans.

Smoke billows from a Freedom Ride bus after it was bombed near Anniston, Alabama.

Victory

The Freedom Ride was delayed, but it would not be stopped. After hearing what had happened, a group of students in Nashville decided to go to Birmingham to continue the trip. Alabama Governor John Patterson promised federal officials that the riders would be protected. Yet when the bus arrived in Montgomery, mobs attacked and started a riot. In Jackson, Mississippi, the riders were arrested at the bus station. They were jailed, but a new group of riders traveled to Jackson to take their place. Over the next few months more than 300 Freedom Riders were arrested.

On a Freedom Ride

James Farmer of CORE, a participant in the Freedom Rides, recalls the trip from Montgomery to Jackson:

We got to the border between Alabama and Mississippi and saw that famous sign, "Welcome to the Magnolia State," and our hearts jumped into our mouths.... There were Mississippi National Guardsmen flanking the highway with their guns pointed toward the forest on both sides of the road.... As we got to the suburbs of Jackson, one of the Freedom Riders broke into song, and this was as it had to be. His words went something like this:

> *I'm taking a ride on the Greyhound bus line,*
> *I'm a-riding the front seat to Jackson this time.*
> *Hallelujah, I'm a-travelin',*
> *Hallelujah, ain't it fine?*
> *Hallelujah, I'm a-travelin',*
> *Down Freedom's main line.*

Like the sit-ins, the Freedom Rides helped win more people over to the civil rights cause. They also led to an important victory. While the rides were taking place, Attorney General Robert Kennedy urged the Interstate Commerce Commission (ICC), the federal agency that regulates travel between the states, to take action. In September 1961 the ICC banned segregation in interstate travel.

Birmingham

Fred Shuttlesworth leads a meeting of civil rights activists preparing for protests in Birmingham, Alabama.

As the civil rights movement gained speed, its leaders decided to take a bold step. They would launch coordinated, full-scale protests in places where racism and discrimination were strongest. They were determined to fight segregation in the places where the sit-ins, Freedom Rides, and other campaigns had met the strongest resistance. In 1963 they targeted Birmingham, the largest city in Alabama.

A center of segregation

In the early 1960s, Birmingham was considered the most segregated city in the United States. The savage beatings of Freedom Riders in 1961 was only one example of its history of racist violence. The threat to blacks was so great that many of them called the city "Bombingham." The city's public officials were hostile as well. The commissioner of public safety, Eugene "Bull" Connor, was one of Birmingham's most well-known racists. As head of both the police and fire departments, he made no effort to hide his support for segregation. Some of the police officers under his command belonged to the Ku Klux Klan.

Despite this hostile environment, civil rights activists had been fighting against segregation in Birmingham for years. They were led by Fred Shuttlesworth, a minister and one of the founders of the SCLC. In 1963, Shuttlesworth decided that Birmingham should be the site of SCLC's next major campaign. Martin Luther King Jr., Ralph Abernathy, and other SCLC leaders agreed. Their goal would be to end all forms of segregation and racial discrimination in the city.

Lessons from Albany

The SCLC knew that Birmingham would be its biggest challenge yet. They remembered very well what had happened not long before in a similar campaign in Albany, Georgia. From December 1961 to August 1962, the SCLC and SNCC had joined forces with local groups in Albany to hold sit-ins, boycotts, and marches. But the campaign, known as the Albany Movement, ended without having made much progress.

The SCLC learned from the disappointment of the Albany Movement. Its leaders realized that the campaign suffered from a lack of focus. Many of the people who took part were inexperienced, and they had failed to set clear goals. This mistake would not be repeated. The SCLC planned carefully for Birmingham. Their overall strategy was to target the city's downtown businesses.

The campaign

The Birmingham campaign began on April 3, 1963. The protests included boycotts, sit-ins, picketing, and marches to city hall. Bull Connor responded by getting an Alabama court to ban more than 100 civil rights activists from taking part in any protests. Among them was King. When he disobeyed the order by leading a march, he was arrested and jailed. While imprisoned, King wrote what became known as "Letter from Birmingham Jail." In it King defended the tactics of nonviolence and argued that the fight against segregation could wait no longer.

Firefighters use their hoses to brutally knock down protesters in the streets of Birmingham.

After King was released from jail, he joined in planning the next phase of the campaign. The SCLC decided to get children involved in the protests. On May 2, 1963, more than 1,000 students marched through the streets of Birmingham. Some were as young as six years old. The children sang, chanted slogans, and prayed as the police arrested them. By the end of the day, hundreds had been put in jail. When the protests continued the next day, Bull Connor ordered police officers to use their attack dogs against the children. At the same time, firefighters turned their powerful hoses on the protesters. The force of the water knocked the children down in the street and rammed them into walls. Television coverage of the brutal treatment of the children horrified Americans.

As the protests continued, Birmingham's business leaders began to discuss with the SCLC. On May 10 a deal was announced. The business leaders agreed to desegregate their stores and hire black workers. The agreement was a breakthrough for Birmingham. It also had a much wider impact. During the summer of 1963, blacks of all ages protested throughout the South on a scale never before seen.

Political Responses to the Movement

The 1963 protests showed that in the civil rights struggle there was no turning back. Although resistance was still strong in parts of the South, the movement had won the sympathy of millions of Americans. The growing pressure for change finally forced the federal government to get more involved in civil rights issues.

Blacks and whites work together at a New Deal building project in New York City in the late 1930s.

Mixed record

For years, the progress of the movement was slowed by the federal government's failure to give it full support. This does not necessarily mean, however, that the presidents of the time opposed equality for blacks. Often a president's handling of civil rights issues had less to do with his personal feelings than with politics. Sometimes the president was afraid to get involved because his actions were sure to lose him supporters on one side of the issue or the other.

Largely because of these political concerns, the federal government's support for the civil rights struggle had been mixed. During the 1930s, President Roosevelt began many programs to help the United States out of the economic crisis known as the Great Depression. These programs, called the New Deal, helped both blacks and whites by giving them jobs and valuable aid. Roosevelt also named more blacks to leadership positions within his government than any president before him. Yet many blacks faulted Roosevelt for failing to take a strong position in favor of racial equality. He failed to speak out, for example, when Congress refused to pass laws against lynching. He was afraid of losing the support of Southern lawmakers.

The movement made progress under the next two presidents, Harry S Truman and Dwight D. Eisenhower, in the late 1940s and the 1950s. But they, too, were worried about the political effects of their actions. Truman took a major step by creating the Committee on Civil Rights in 1946. Nevertheless, he was still somewhat hesitant to act because of opposition from Southern politicians. When he needed the support of Northerners to get elected in 1948, though, he decided to take a stronger stance in favor of civil rights. This move lost him the support of Southerners in his party, but he won the election anyway. Soon afterward, Truman banned segregation in the armed forces. In 1957, while Eisenhower was president, Congress passed the country's first civil rights law since 1875. Yet Eisenhower failed to voice support for the Supreme Court's *Brown* ruling. When the conflict over school integration arose at Central High in Little Rock in 1957, Eisenhower hoped to avoid getting involved. Eventually, however, mob violence and Arkansas Governor Faubus' resistance to the federal government forced the president into action.

FBI

One federal agency earned a reputation for actively working against the civil rights movement. The Federal Bureau of Investigation (FBI) is the leading crime-fighting force in the United States. For nearly 50 years—from 1924 to 1972—the FBI was led by a man named J. Edgar Hoover. He accused Martin Luther King Jr. and other civil rights leaders of being communist troublemakers. At the time, the leading enemy of the United States was the Soviet Union, which had a communist government.

Under Hoover's leadership, the FBI treated all civil rights activists with suspicion. The agency investigated the movement as if it was somehow a threat to the security of the United States. The main target was King. FBI agents followed his every move and secretly listened to his phone conversations. At the same time, the FBI did little to stop the ongoing violence against blacks.

Kennedy administration

When John F. Kennedy was elected president in 1960, civil rights activists believed that they would finally get the full support of the federal government. Just before the election, Kennedy made a move that helped him win the support of many black voters. After Martin Luther King Jr. was arrested during a sit-in in Atlanta, Georgia, Kennedy and his brother Robert helped get him out of jail. Unfortunately, the blacks who helped elect Kennedy were soon disappointed. In addition to the support of blacks, Kennedy had also depended heavily on the votes of white Southerners to get elected. Like the presidents before him, Kennedy faced a difficult political situation. He responded by putting forth only a modest civil rights program.

President John F. Kennedy developed into an important political supporter for the civil rights movement.

Soon, however, events forced Kennedy to take action. The violence during the Freedom Rides was a great embarrassment for the president and Robert Kennedy, the attorney general. The United States held itself up to the world as an example of democracy, but it treated millions of its own people as second-class citizens. Then came the massive demonstrations in Birmingham and other cities in 1963. These protests urged both John and Robert Kennedy to get deeply involved in civil rights issues for the first time.

March on Washington and the Civil Rights Act

Hundreds of thousands participate in the March on Washington, an historic display of public support for the civil rights movement.

On June 11, 1963, while demonstrations continued across the South, President Kennedy went on television to talk to the nation about the civil rights movement. His speech was the most powerful statement on the issue by any U.S. president up to then. "We are confronted primarily with a moral issue," he said. "It is as old as the Scriptures and is as clear as the American Constitution. The heart of the question is whether all Americans are to be afforded equal rights and equal opportunities; whether we are going to treat our fellow Americans as we want to be treated." He proposed historic civil rights legislation aimed at ending racial discrimination once and for all. Before Kennedy's proposal could become law, it had to be approved by Congress.

The march

Civil rights leaders saw Kennedy's speech as a chance to make a major statement. Months before the speech, union leader A. Philip Randolph had revived his idea of a massive march in Washington, D.C. In 1941, Randolph had planned such a march to protest job discrimination in the defense industries, but he called it off when President Roosevelt agreed to his demands. Nearly twenty years later, Randolph was still concerned with the limited economic opportunities for blacks. Many more blacks than whites were unemployed, and the wages of working blacks were still less than those of whites. Working with fellow activist Bayard Rustin, Randolph began planning an event called the "March on Washington for Jobs and Freedom." After Kennedy's speech, other civil rights leaders joined in the planning. They expanded the scope of the march beyond Randolph's focus on economic opportunities. The overall goal was to urge Congress to pass Kennedy's civil rights bill.

At first Kennedy tried to talk civil rights leaders out of the march. He warned them that the march could fail by making Southern congressmen even more determined to keep the bill from being passed. He also feared that such a large gathering could lead to violence. But the civil rights leaders told him that the march would go on. They also assured him that they were planning very carefully to make sure that the march would be peaceful. Seeing that he could not stop the march, Kennedy put his support behind it.

More than 250,000 people gathered for the March on Washington on August 28, 1963. They were watched closely by thousands of police officers and National Guard troops, but the march was as peaceful as the leaders had promised. The crowd first marched from the Washington Monument to the Lincoln Memorial. There they listened to speeches by civil rights leaders and songs by famous entertainers. The highlight of the day was Martin Luther King Jr.'s "I Have a Dream" speech. "I have a dream," he said, "that my four little children will one day live in a nation where they will not be judged by the color of their skin but by the content of their character." His speech was broadcast live on television to an audience of millions.

Martin Luther King Jr. waves to the huge crowd during the March on Washington.

Civil Rights Act

The March on Washington was a powerful display of the widespread support for the civil rights cause. Nevertheless, President Kennedy still struggled to get his civil rights bill passed by Congress. The bill was stalled when Kennedy was assassinated in November 1963. Civil rights leaders feared that Kennedy's death would mean the death of the bill as well. But the new president, Lyndon B. Johnson, took up the civil rights cause where Kennedy left off. He proposed an even stronger civil rights bill and worked hard to get it passed. After many months of debate in Congress, Johnson signed the Civil Rights Act into law on July 2, 1964. Among many other things, the act banned discrimination in employment and public facilities. It finally put the full force of the federal government behind the civil rights cause.

Struggle in Mississippi

The Civil Rights Act accomplished a lot, but it was not perfect. One major weakness in the law was its lack of a strong guarantee of voting rights. Another was its failure to protect people from racist violence. But perhaps the biggest problem was one that no law could solve—it could not change people's minds. Making racial discrimination illegal did not make stubborn racists any more willing to treat blacks as equals. The struggle for civil rights was not yet over. Nowhere was this clearer than in the state of Mississippi.

The challenge

While Birmingham, Alabama, was thought to be the most segregated city in the United States, Mississippi was widely considered to be the most segregated state. Several high-profile events in the 1950s and 1960s helped earn Mississippi this reputation. In 1955, a fourteen-year-old black boy named Emmett Till was kidnapped and murdered in Money, Mississippi. The only reason for the brutal crime was that Emmett supposedly whistled at a white woman. The murder made the national news, unlike hundreds of other murders committed against blacks in the state.

An SNCC worker helps a Mississippi man register to vote during a drive in the early 1960s.

In 1962, Mississippi attracted national attention again when James Meredith became the first black student to enter the University of Mississippi. President Kennedy had to send federal troops to restore order when whites responded by rioting. Federal marshals stayed on campus to protect Meredith until he graduated. Another racial murder put Mississippi in the spotlight in 1963. Medgar Evers, an NAACP worker, was shot to death outside of his home in the city of Jackson. The Civil Rights Act made little difference in the lives of Mississippi's blacks. Most of them were too afraid of white violence to test the law. Most schools remained segregated, and only a small number of blacks registered to vote.

Voter registration drives

Long before the Civil Rights Act was passed, activists had realized the importance of getting Mississippi's blacks to vote. The state had a large black population, but in the early 1960s, only about five percent of the black residents were registered to vote. If blacks voted in greater numbers, their political power could be significant. They could vote the racists out of office and finally bring real change to the state.

Progress in registering Mississippi's blacks to vote was slow. The NAACP worked on the project for years with limited success. In 1961, SNCC began a registration drive in the state, but white violence forced the group out after a few months. The next year SNCC returned to Mississippi, this time with the support of CORE, SCLC, and the NAACP. The united group, called the Council of Federated Organizations (COFO), expanded the voter registration project.

In the fall of 1963, COFO put together an event called Freedom Vote. The group held a mock election for blacks who could not vote in the real election for state governor. About 80 white students from the North came to Mississippi to help organize the event. On "election day," more than 80,000 blacks cast votes across the state.

Freedom Summer
Encouraged by the Freedom Vote, COFO planned a huge voter registration drive for the summer of 1964. The goal of the new project, called Freedom Summer, was to prepare blacks for the upcoming presidential election. Seeing that the white students drew much attention to Freedom Vote, the COFO organizers invited more students to take part in Freedom Summer. Hundreds of students came to the South from some of the finest schools in the country. They helped set up "freedom schools" to teach people about black history and their rights as citizens.

Is this America, the land of the free and the home of the brave? Where we have to sleep with our telephones off the hook because our lives are threatened daily, because we want to live as decent human beings in America?

—Fannie Lou Hamer, speaking at the 1964 Democratic National Convention

The students met strong resistance. While the first group of students was still arriving, three civil rights workers disappeared. One was black and two were white. They were found dead more than a month later. Widespread anger over the murders led President Johnson to take action. He finally forced the FBI to tackle the Ku Klux Klan and other violent groups.

Freedom Summer also led to the creation of a new political party. COFO organized the Mississippi Freedom Democratic Party (MFDP) because blacks were shut out of the state's regular Democratic Party. The MFDP sent a group of mostly black delegates to the Democratic National Convention in Atlantic City, New Jersey. Fannie Lou Hamer, a sharecropper and leader of the MFDP, spoke before the convention about the hardships of Mississippi's blacks. Her powerful speech was broadcast nationwide. The Democrats, led by President Johnson, offered to accept only two of the party's 68 delegates. Angry and disappointed, the MFDP refused the offer. In future years, however, the state's delegates were chosen more fairly.

Selma and the Voting Rights Act

The voting rights effort in Mississippi was part of a larger, ongoing struggle throughout the South. Freedom Summer helped speed up the slow but steady progress that had been made over the years by the NAACP and other groups. By 1964, about 42 percent of adult blacks in the South were registered to vote. This was a great improvement over the 3 percent registered in 1940.

Nevertheless, the rate of voter registration among Southern blacks still lagged behind that of whites. To keep blacks from voting, racist officials used the same methods they had used for years. They made voters pay a poll tax, which many poor blacks could not afford. They also required voters to pass difficult tests. Many Southern blacks could not pass tests requiring reading and writing because they had been denied a decent education. Yet educated blacks failed the tests as well. Even if they did well on the tests, the people in charge of registration would say they failed. Along with these methods, whites continued to use threats and violence to keep blacks from registering.

Alabama state troopers use tear gas against marchers at the Edmund Pettus Bridge on March 7, 1965.

Selma campaign

Civil rights leaders felt that they needed to make a bold move in support of voting rights. The SCLC chose Selma, Alabama, as the site of a massive registration campaign. Like Birmingham in 1963, Selma was targeted because of its reputation as a tough city. Only about two percent of the city's 15,000 blacks of voting age were registered. The city's sheriff, Jim Clark, was a segregationist with a history of rough hostility against blacks. Also, Alabama overall had remained hostile to desegregation even after the Birmingham campaign. In September 1963, just weeks after the March on Washington, whites bombed a Baptist church in Birmingham, killing four black girls. Alabama's governor, George Wallace, was a national symbol for racism. He was known for the slogan "Segregation now! Segregation tomorrow! Segregation forever!"

The SCLC began its Selma campaign in January 1965. Martin Luther King Jr. led a march to Selma's courthouse. A few days later, Selma's black schoolteachers held their own march. As respected members of the community, they set an example that many others followed. The marches quickly grew in number. In early February King and hundreds of other marchers were arrested and jailed. Among them were many schoolchildren. Selma stayed in the headlines after a state trooper shot and killed a young black protester, Jimmie Lee Jackson, in a nearby town.

Jackson's death inspired SCLC leaders to plan a march from Selma to Montgomery, the state capital. They wanted to face Governor Wallace in person. About 600 people gathered for the 54-mile (87-kilometer) march on Sunday, March 7. They did not get far. When they reached the Edmund Pettus Bridge, they were met by Sheriff Clark and hundreds of Alabama state troopers. The marchers halted, but they did not leave. Then the troopers attacked. They used clubs and whips and shot tear gas into the crowd. Some chased the marchers back to Selma, clubbing them along the way. Dozens of marchers were severely hurt. The day came to be known as "Bloody Sunday."

Martin Luther King Jr. leads thousands of demonstrators on the last part of the march from Selma to Montgomery on March 26, 1965.

Television and newspaper coverage of the incident horrified Americans. When the march to Montgomery began anew on March 21, many whites were among the participants. This time the marchers were protected by federal troops. Along the way the march increased to about 25,000 people. Upon reaching Montgomery on March 25, all shared in the victory.

Voting Rights Act

Meanwhile, President Johnson had proposed a strong law guaranteeing voting rights. In a powerful televised speech, he urged Congress to act quickly in support of his Voting Rights Act. "This time, on this issue," he said, "there must be no delay, or no hesitation, or no compromise." A few weeks later Congress passed the act. On August 6, 1965, Johnson signed it into law.

The Voting Rights Act was the climax of the civil rights movement. The historic law took the authority for registering voters out of the hands of the states and gave it to federal officials instead. With great numbers of blacks finally able to register and vote, racist officials were voted out of office throughout the South. The system of segregation finally collapsed.

President Johnson reacts

What happened in Selma is part of a larger movement which reaches into every section and every state in America. It is the effort of American Negroes to secure for themselves the full blessings of American life. Their cause must be our cause, too. Because it's not just Negroes, but really it's all of us who must overcome the crippling legacy of bigotry and injustice. And we shall overcome.

—President Johnson, in his speech proposing the Voting Rights Act on March 15, 1965

Civil Rights and the Arts

President Johnson's speech proposing the Voting Rights Act was especially moving to many people because of the words he chose to end it. "We shall overcome," he said, using the title of a song that had become a theme of the civil rights movement. "Oh, deep in my heart," the song went, "I do believe, we shall overcome someday." Singing "We Shall Overcome" and other "freedom songs" helped bring people together and raise their spirits as they took part in marches, sit-ins, and other protests. "In a sense," said Martin Luther King Jr., "the freedom songs are the soul of the movement."

"We Shall Overcome" began as an old Baptist hymn called "I'll Overcome Someday." In the 1940s, black union workers sang the song as they walked the picket lines during a strike. Folk singers learned the song from the strikers and changed the words to "We Shall Overcome." These singers taught the song to young civil rights activists, especially from the SNCC. In the 1960s, the song swept the country. Eventually it became a part of movements for peace and justice all over the world.

Supporting the cause

The story behind "We Shall Overcome" is just one example of how popular performers—both black and white—helped advance the civil rights cause. From the start singers, actors, and other entertainers contributed their talents to the movement. Black performers did so while battling racial discrimination themselves. In the movies and on television, good roles for black actors were hard to find. The few parts that were available to blacks often reflected and added to racial stereotypes. Black actors played parts such as convicts, servants, and chorus members. Accurate portraits of black life and culture were rare. In the world of music, black singers and musicians were not allowed to perform in certain places because of their race. When they were able to perform, their audiences were often segregated.

Opera singer Marian Anderson is congratulated by government minister Harold Ickes after her concert on the steps of the Lincoln Memorial in 1939.

Despite these obstacles, a number of black performers were able to become famous in the entertainment industry. In the process, they often used their fame to call attention to the conditions blacks faced. One of the earliest such performers was Paul Robeson. A man of many talents, Robeson became an international star in the 1920s. He did not settle for the stereotypical roles that black actors were usually given. He acted in plays, starred in movies, and gave concerts in the United States and Europe. Robeson also spoke out about inequality both in the entertainment industry and in the United States in general. The NAACP recognized his efforts in 1945 by awarding him its highest honor, the Spingarn Medal.

Black opera singer Marian Anderson also found success in the face of racial discrimination. Although she was already very successful in Europe, she was barred from giving a concert at Constitution Hall in Washington, D.C., in 1939. Anderson instead performed outdoors at the Lincoln Memorial on Easter Sunday. More than 75,000 people attended the concert. In 1955, Anderson became the first black singer to perform at the famous Metropolitan Opera Company in New York. She received the Spingarn Medal in 1939.

Celebrity support for the civil rights movement probably reached its height at the March on Washington in 1963. A number of famous entertainers took part in the event, some performing for the crowd. Among them were the actors Sidney Poitier, Marlon Brando, and Paul Newman and the singers Harry Belafonte, Lena Horne, Mahalia Jackson, and Bob Dylan. Marian Anderson, returning to the site of her historic 1939 concert, sang "He's Got the Whole World in His Hands." And folksinger Joan Baez led the crowd in singing "We Shall Overcome."

Sammy Davis Jr. was one of many entertainers, both African American and white, who appeared at the March on Washington and supported the civil rights movement.

"Strange Fruit"

Written by a New York schoolteacher named Abel Meeropol, the song "Strange Fruit" was made popular by jazz singer Billie Holliday in 1939. It is a powerful statement against lynching and racism in general.

> Southern trees bear a strange fruit,
> Blood on the leaves and blood at the root,
> Black bodies swinging in the Southern breeze,
> Strange fruit hanging from the poplar trees.
>
> Pastoral scene of the gallant South,
> The bulging eyes and the twisted mouth,
> Scent of magnolia sweet and fresh,
> Then the sudden smell of burning flesh.
>
> Here is a fruit for the crows to pluck,
> For the rain to gather, for the wind to suck,
> For the sun to rot, for a tree to drop,
> Here is a strange and bitter crop.

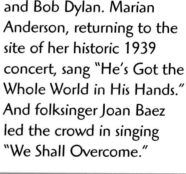

A New Direction

All through the events of the 1950s and 1960s, some blacks continued to believe that the goal of equal treatment was unrealistic. They believed that racism ran too deeply in the United States ever to allow for true equality. In the mid-1960s, increasing numbers of blacks began to feel this way. Despite the passage of the Civil Rights Act and the Voting Rights Act, they were disappointed with the progress of the civil rights movement. The victories of the movement had done little to improve their daily lives. In both the South and the North, many blacks still lived in poverty. They were still shut out of good housing and jobs. The unemployment rate among blacks was twice as high as the rate for whites.

A burning store collapses during the Watts riots in Los Angeles in 1965.

Continuing racial discrimination led to mounting tensions between blacks and whites, especially in cities. In the mid-1960s, these tensions erupted into riots. In August 1965, just days after the Voting Rights Act became law, the arrest of a young black driver set off six days of violence in the black section of Los Angeles called Watts. Thousands of people were arrested, and 34 were killed. In the summer of 1967 riots broke out again, this time in more than 100 cities. The most serious riots killed dozens of people in Newark, New Jersey, and Detroit, Michigan.

Malcolm X and his influence

The frustration that led to the riots also caused many blacks to give up on the civil rights movement. Deciding that the strategy of nonviolence was not working, they looked for new ideas. Many united around the leadership of Malcolm X. In the late 1950s, Malcolm X emerged as an alternative to Martin Luther King Jr. A bold and intense speaker, he rejected nonviolence and said that blacks should achieve justice "by any means necessary." By this he meant that blacks should answer white violence with violence of their own. Malcolm X also rejected integration and urged blacks to take pride in their race. By the time he was killed by rivals in 1964, he had softened his anti-white message. But many blacks clung to his original ideas of racial separation. The more challenging atmosphere of the mid-1960s led to changes in some civil rights groups and the creation of new organizations. One of the existing groups that changed its focus was SNCC. The group's difficult experiences in Mississippi during Freedom Summer in 1964 caused its black members to lose faith in whites. In 1965, SNCC expelled all whites from the organization. In Alabama the next year, SNCC formed a local political party with a growling black panther as its symbol. The party was meant to represent blacks in a way that the existing parties could not. Months later, young blacks in Oakland, California, started the Black Panther Party, which attracted followers nationwide.

A name for the new movement emerged during a protest march through Mississippi in June 1966. The organizer of the event was James Meredith, who had made history four years earlier as the first black student to enter the University of Mississippi. During the march, SNCC leader Stokely Carmichael urged a crowd to call for "black power." The term quickly caught on nationwide.

Activists raise their fists in support of black power at a rally for the Black Panther Party.

King's last efforts

As the black power movement became more popular, Martin Luther King Jr. stuck to the ideals of nonviolence. Yet even King's activism took on a different tone. King and the SCLC realized that the civil rights movement had to change people's lives, not just the laws. With this in mind, King brought the movement to the North in 1966 with a campaign against housing discrimination in Chicago. King and his fellow marchers were met by mobs of angry whites as bad as any they had seen in the South. Eventually the Chicago city government agreed to support housing integration, but little change actually came about.

In late 1967, King announced an SCLC plan to bring poor people of all races to Washington, D.C., in a protest against poverty. The event was to be known as the Poor People's Campaign. Protesters would camp out in the capital until the government took action. During the

Nobody can give you freedom. Nobody can give you equality or justice or anything. If you're a man, you take it.

—Malcolm X

planning for the campaign, King traveled to Memphis, Tennessee, to support a strike by garbage workers. On April 4, 1968, he was shot and killed as he stood on the balcony of his motel. King's assassination led to riots across the nation. It also marked the end of the civil rights movement as a united effort. The Poor People's Campaign went on without him, but it was not a success.

Other Civil Rights Struggles

The black civil rights movement inspired activists to push for equal rights for other groups of people. In the 1960s and 1970s, women, American Indians, and Hispanic Americans worked for change.

Women's movement

In the 19th and early 20th centuries, women made progress in narrowing the gaps between the sexes in a number of areas. Many more women started attending college, and they achieved the right to vote in 1920. But in the 1960s, women still faced inequalities, especially in the workplace. They had fewer job opportunities and often were paid less than men for the same work. The Civil Rights Act of 1964 barred discrimination based on sex as well as on race, but many women were not satisfied with its results.

In 1966, women activists formed the National Organization for Women (NOW) to work for equal rights. The group won an important victory when Title IX of the Education Amendments Act became law in 1972. It required colleges that receive federal aid to offer equal educational opportunities to women. That same year Congress approved an amendment to the U.S. Constitution that would have barred all forms of gender discrimination. The Equal Rights Amendment (ERA), however, failed to win the approval of enough states to become law. The failure of the ERA was a disappointment for the women's movement, but NOW and other groups continued to push for equality with men.

American Indians

American Indians had longstanding complaints against the federal government. As white settlers moved westward across the United States in the 19th century, they fought with the American Indians already living on the land. The federal government forced or tricked American Indian tribes into giving up their land through treaties. Sometimes the government promised the American Indians financial aid or schools in return, but often the treaties were ignored. Most American Indians were forced onto reservations, where they lived in poverty. In the 20th century many American Indians moved to cities, but their conditions were not much better.

American Indians proclaim Alcatraz Island to be "United Indian Property" after occupying it in 1969.

In 1968, American Indian activists created a civil rights organization called the American Indian Movement (AIM). The group wanted to force the federal government to pay more attention to the needs of American Indians. Among its most important goals was making the federal government review treaties that were either illegal or ignored. In one famous protest, AIM members and other American Indians took over Alcatraz Island in San Francisco Bay from 1969 to 1971. In 1973, AIM led a group of activists in a takeover of a reservation at Wounded Knee in South Dakota. Wounded Knee was the site of an 1890 confrontation in which U.S. troops massacred more than 200 men, women, and children of the Sioux tribe. After a 71-day standoff with federal marshals, the activists agreed to leave in return for the federal government's promise to review its policies. These events drew national attention to the cause of American Indian rights.

Hispanic Americans

The number of Hispanics living in the United States grew quickly during the 1960s. Many of the newcomers were migrant workers, meaning that they moved from farm to farm picking crops. They worked long hours for little pay. In 1962, Cesar Chavez joined with Dolores Huerta and other activists to organize Mexican and Mexican American farm workers into a union. The group used nonviolent protest in their efforts to improve pay and working conditions on U.S. farms. Eventually the union became the United Farm Workers (UFW). The group launched a strike and a nationwide boycott of California grapes in 1965 to protest unfair treatment of grape pickers in the state. By 1970, many grape growers had agreed to the union's demands.

Cesar Chavez (holding sign) leads a group of people urging support for a boycott of California grapes.

The Movement Continues

The death of Martin Luther King Jr. in 1968 left black Americans shocked and dejected. Yet not even King's murder could undo the progress made by the civil rights movement in the 1950s and 1960s. In the years that followed, many blacks took advantage of newfound opportunities in politics, education, and employment. At the same time, however, continuing inequalities reminded blacks that the struggle was not over.

Measures of progress

As the number of black voters grew, black candidates won political offices all over the country. In 1967, Cleveland, Ohio, became the first major U.S. city to elect a black mayor, Carl Stokes. Since then, black mayors have been elected in many of the nation's largest cities, including New York, Chicago, Los Angeles, Philadelphia, Detroit, Houston, and Atlanta. Black membership in Congress grew as well. In 1971 Congress had only thirteen black representatives. That year, they joined together to form a group called the Congressional Black Caucus (CBC), which committed itself to representing the interests of black Americans. In the early 21st century, the CBC had close to 40 members. All told, the number of black elected officials nationwide increased from 1,469 in 1970 to more than 9,000 in 2000. Probably the best-known black leader to seek political office was Jesse Jackson, who ran for the Democratic nomination for U.S. president in 1984 and 1988. Although he did not win the nominations, his two strong campaigns brought national attention to blacks in United States politics.

Civil Rights leader Jesse Jackson, right, with his son, Jesse Jackson Jr., in 1996 at the Democratic National Convention.

Blacks also made important gains in education. In the late 1960s and early 1970s, federal courts finally forced Southern school boards to stop delaying desegregation. As a result, the number of black students attending integrated schools increased dramatically. In addition, the rate of blacks graduating from high school and college skyrocketed. In 1960, only 20 percent of blacks were high school graduates. By 2000, that number had risen to 79 percent. The rate of college graduation among blacks increased from just 3 percent in 1960 to nearly 17 percent in 2000—more than a fivefold increase.

The civil rights movement also helped blacks improve their economic standing. As job discrimination decreased, many blacks entered middle-class careers that had once shut them out. More and more blacks became doctors, lawyers, engineers, business managers, teachers, nurses, bank tellers, and salesclerks.

Beginning in the late 1960s, the remarkable black advances in higher education and employment received a boost through programs known as affirmative action. Introduced by the government, these programs were meant to make up for past discrimination. Affirmative action gave preference to minorities and women in school admissions and job hiring. The programs helped make the representation of blacks and women closer to that of whites in colleges and jobs.

Members of the Congressional Black Caucaus are sworn in as Congress begins its session in January, 2003.

Ongoing concerns

Despite the progress made by blacks, they continued to lag behind whites in many areas. One example is income. As the size of the black middle class grew, the gap between the incomes of white and black workers narrowed. Nevertheless, at the start of the 21st century, blacks on average still earned only about 70 percent of what whites earned. On top of this, the gains in jobs and income left behind many blacks altogether. In the early 21st century, more than 20 percent of blacks lived in poverty, more than twice the rate of whites. Blacks were also more than twice as likely as whites to be unemployed.

Even as many blacks continued to struggle, affirmative action programs came under attack. Some whites argued that favoring blacks for college admissions and jobs on the basis of race was reverse discrimination. They challenged affirmative action in the courts, and in the 1980s the Supreme Court significantly weakened the programs. In the second half of the 1990s, several states passed laws that barred government institutions from using race as a factor in hiring. Schools in some places were forbidden from considering race in admissions decisions as well. Challenges to affirmative action continued into the 21st century.

Martin Luther King Jr. Day

Martin Luther King Jr. was honored in a number of ways after his death in 1968. Perhaps the most notable tribute was the creation of a national holiday in his honor. In 1983, Congress voted to make the third Monday in January Martin Luther King Jr. Day. King was the first black American to be honored in this way. The holiday was first celebrated in 1986.

The victories of the 1950s and 1960s were real and remarkable. But the work of preserving and building on those gains continues today.

Timeline of the Civil Rights Movement

1905	W.E.B. Du Bois and other black professionals form a group called the Niagara Movement to work for civil rights
1909	Blacks and whites together form the National Association for the Advancement of Colored People (NAACP)
1942	The interracial Congress of Racial Equality (CORE) is founded in Chicago, Illinois, and holds the first sit-ins
1947	CORE organizes the first Freedom Ride through the South
1948	President Truman orders an end to racial discrimination in the armed forces
1954	In the case *Brown v. Board of Education of Topeka,* the Supreme Court rules that racial segregation in public schools is unconstitutional
1955	Emmett Till, a fourteen-year-old boy from Chicago, is kidnapped and murdered in Mississippi
	Martin Luther King Jr. leads a boycott of segregated city buses in Montgomery, Alabama
1957	President Eisenhower sends federal troops to escort nine black students into Central High School in Little Rock, Arkansas
	Martin Luther King Jr. and other Southern black ministers form the Southern Christian Leadership Conference (SCLC)
1960	The sit-in movement begins in Greensboro, North Carolina, with a protest by four students from North Carolina Agricultural and Technical College
	Black and white students form the Student Nonviolent Coordinating Committee (SNCC) to organize civil rights protests
1961	CORE begins a series of Freedom Rides through the South
	SNCC begins its first voter registration drive in Mississippi
	The SCLC and SNCC launch the Albany Movement, a civil rights campaign in Albany, Georgia
1962	Riots break out when James Meredith becomes the first black student to enter the University of Mississippi
1963	The SCLC conducts a massive civil rights campaign in Birmingham, Alabama
	Medgar Evers, an NAACP leader in Mississippi, is killed outside his home
	More then 250,000 people take part in the March on Washington, in which Martin Luther King Jr. delivers his "I Have a Dream" speech
	A Baptist church is bombed in Birmingham, killing four black girls

1964	President Johnson signs the Civil Rights Act into law
	SNCC leads a huge voter registration drive in Mississippi called Freedom Summer
	The newly formed Mississippi Freedom Democratic Party (MFDP) sends representatives to the Democratic National Convention in Atlantic City, New Jersey
	Martin Luther King Jr. is awarded the Nobel Prize for Peace
1965	The SCLC launches a voter registration drive in Selma, Alabama, and protesters march from Selma to Montgomery, the state capital
	President Johnson signs the Voting Rights Act
	Blacks riot in the Watts section of Los Angeles, California
1966	James Meredith leads a protest march through Mississippi, and during the march SNCC leader Stokely Carmichael introduces the slogan "black power"
	Martin Luther King Jr. begins a campaign against housing discrimination in Chicago, Illinois
	The Black Panther Party is founded in Oakland, California
1967	Carl Stokes is elected mayor of Cleveland, Ohio, the first black to be elected mayor of a major U.S. city
1968	Martin Luther King Jr. is assassinated in Memphis, Tennessee
	Ralph Abernathy leads the Poor People's March in Washington, D.C.

Further Reading

Claybourne, Anna. *Martin Luther King Jr., Civil Rights Hero.* Austin, Tex.: Raintree Publishers, 2001.

Kallen, Stuart A. *The Civil Rights Movement.* Edina, Minn.: ABDO Publishing Company, 2001.

Meltzer, Milton. *There Comes a Time: The Struggle for Civil Rights.* New York: Random House Children's Books, 2002.

Somerlott, Robert. *The Little Rock School Desegregation Crisis in American History.* Berkeley Heights, N.J.: Enslow Publishers, 2001.

Steele, Philip. *Rosa Parks and Her Protest for Civil Rights.* North Mankato, Minn.: Smart Apple Media, 2002.

Walsh, Frank. *The Montgomery Bus Boycott.* Milwaukee, Wisc.: Gareth Stevens, 2003.

Glossary

accommodation dealing with segregation by adapting to it instead of trying to change it

activism action taken in support of a cause. A person that practices activism is an *activist*.

affirmative action program designed to make up for past discrimination by improving educational and employment opportunities of women and minorities

amendment addition or change to a document such as a constitution

assassinate murder suddenly, especially a public figure

attorney general chief law officer of a country or state; in the United States, the head of the Department of Justice

boycott refusal to do business with a company or organization, often in the hope of changing its policies

citizen person who owes loyalty to the place he or she lives in return for certain rights and benefits

Civil War war fought in the U.S from 1861 to 1865 between the Union (North) and Confederate (South) states over issues of slavery and states' rights

COFO Council of Federated Organizations; united group—consisting of SNCC, CORE, SCLC, NAACP—formed in 1962 that expanded the SNCC voter registration project in Mississippi.

communism social system in which property and goods are held in common. A person who believes in communism is a *communist*.

Congress lawmaking body of the U.S. government

constitution document that describes a government's functions and limits

CORE Congress of Racial Equality; James Farmer founded CORE in Chicago in 1942. The group's goal was to end racial discrimination through nonviolence.

delegate representative sent to a convention or other meeting; in the United States, delegates from each state choose the candidates for president every four years

direct action use of protests to bring about change

discrimination unfair treatment based on characteristics such as race, age, or sex

economy use or management of money

equality state of being equal; having the same status and rights

facility building or equipment that makes an action, operation, or activity easier

FBI Federal Bureau of Investigation; federal agency that earned a reputation for actively working against the civil rights movement

federal describing a union of states that share a government

ghetto part of a city where members of a minority group live, often not by choice but instead because of economic reasons

Great Depression worldwide economic slump that lasted from about 1929 to 1939

harass threaten and bother

immigrant person who comes to a foreign country to live

inequality state of being unequal; groups having more status and rights than others

inferior situated lower down, such as in place or importance

integration opening up an organization or place to people of different groups, such as races

intolerant not accepting of

issue officially giving out or making available

Jim Crow system of laws and customs that kept blacks and whites apart in the southern United States from the 1870s to about the 1950s

Ku Klux Klan terrorist organization formed in 1865; to maintain their sense of superiority over blacks—and the advantages it gave them—the KKK tried to stop black progress through threats and violence

legislature government body with the power to make laws

lynching mob killing of a person who has not been tried or convicted of a crime

mail fraud trying to trick or deceive someone through the mail

MFDP Mississippi Freedom Democratic Party; organization formed by COFO because blacks were shut out of the state's regular Democratic Party

migrant person that moves from one country or region to another

NAACP National Association for the Advancement of Colored People; formed in 1908, the NAACP decided to push for civil rights through lawsuits, not protests

Negro member of the black race identified by physical characteristics; member of a people belonging to the African branch of the black race

New Deal government programs introduced by President Roosevelt in the 1930s to help pull the United States out of the Great Depression

nonviolence working for political and social change using only peaceful ways

poll tax fee that a person must pay in order to vote

public school school that is supported by taxes and run by a local government

racism belief that people of some races are inferior. A person who believes in racism is called a *racist.*

Reconstruction period in U.S. history following the Civil War, lasting from about 1865 to 1877; during this time the country tried to deal with the problems that led to the war and the new problems the end of the war created

registration process by which a person becomes eligible to vote

resolution act of answering or solving

reverse discrimination unfair treatment of a majority group, such as whites

riot public disturbance caused by a crowd of people

SCLC Southern Christian Leadership Conference; formed by a group of black ministers from across the South in 1957. Like CORE, it dedicated itself to working for desegregation and civil rights through nonviolent resistance.

segregation separating people on the basis of a characteristic such as race. A person who believes in segregation is a *segregationist.*

seminary school for the training of priests, ministers, or rabbis

sharecropper farmer who works on land owned by someone else in return for a portion of the crop

SNCC Student Nonviolent Coordinating Committee; formed in 1960, by students of the sit-in movement to organize their protests

standoff when two sides compete but neither can gain an advantage

stereotype widely shared opinion that is accepted without closely considering its basis in fact or admitting there are exceptions

superior situated higher up in rank, importance, or quality

Supreme Court highest court of the U.S., consisting of a chief justice and eight associate justices

terrorist person that uses threats or violence as a means of forcing others to do what one wishes

unconstitutional violating the ideas in a constitution

union organization of workers who band together in support of their common interests, such as fair wages and working conditions

white supremacy belief that white people are superior to people of other races

World War I war fought in Europe from 1914 to 1918 between the Allies (France, Great Britain, Russia, and the U.S.) and Germany and Austria-Hungary over power issues in Europe

World War II war fought in Europe and the Far East from 1939 to 1945 between the Allies (France, Great Britain, Russia, and the U.S.) and the Axis (Germany, Italy, and Japan) over Axis countries' quest for more land

Index